# LEMURIAN SEEDS

## Hope for Humanity

Shelley Kaehr, Ph.D.

# LEMURIAN SEEDS

## Hope for Humanity

Shelley Kaehr, Ph.D.

FIRST EDITION
First Printing, 2006

Cover design by Shelley Kaehr
Photos © Shelley Kaehr

Library of Congress Control Number: 2006905270

Kaehr, Shelley A., 1967—
Lemurian Seeds: Hope for Humanity /
Shelley Kaehr — 1st ed.
p. cm.
Includes bibliographical references.
ISBN: 0-9777556-0-6

An Out of This World Production does not have any authority concerning private business transactions between our authors and the public. If you wish to contact the author or would like more information about this book, please write to the author in care of An Out of This World Production and we will forward your request. Please write to:

Shelley Kaehr, Ph.D.
c/o An Out of This World Production
P.O. Box 610943
Dallas, TX 75261-0943

**www.outofthisworldpublishing.com**

**Also by Shelley Kaehr, Ph.D.**

**Books**

*Just Write It: Step by Step Guide to Writing and Publishing Your First Book*
*Divination of God: Ancient Tool of Prophecy Revealed*
*Edgar Cayce's Guide to Gemstones, Minerals, Metals & More*
*Beyond Reality: Evidence of Parallel Universes*
*Galactic Healing*
*Lifestream: Journeys into Past & Future Lives*
*Gemstone Journeys*
*Origins of Huna: Secret Behind the Secret Science*

**CD's**

*Lifestream: Journey into Past & Future Lives*
*Journey to Spirit: Meeting Your Guides*
*Journey to Spirit: Abundance*
*Journey to Grief Recovery*
*Origins of Huna: Ho'oponopono Cord Cutting*
*Galactic Healing: Healing with the Elements*
*Sacred Sounds*

**DVD's**

*Gemstone Journeys: Laying-on-of-Stones*
*Stones of Power*

# Contents

# Acknowledgements

To Barbara, Geri and Mary Ann for opening me to the idea of Lemurians at this time

To Johanna for giving me my first beautiful Lemurian wand

To Jane Li for your daily inspiration

To Karen for preparing the tools

To Kayse for your continued support

To Will for giving me the key

To Pat for encouraging me

To Tammy for creating the space

To Mickey Gail & Mark for believing in me

# Introduction

I've finally been guided to write about quartz crystals.

Most of my work is with the colored stones which I have always had a special rapport with, but lately I've been drawn to work with special Lemurian Seed crystals.

Some of the information I received about these relatively recent discoveries has led me to write this book. The time is now for this information to get out to a larger audience so that the stones can assist us in fulfilling our destiny.

You know the old saying that God gives us everything we need?

I believe it's true, but I also wonder why, if we already have everything, we are still able to constantly discover new things.

You may have heard recently in the news about a brand new animal species discovered on a remote island. It is incredible that just as we begin to think we've seen it all, we can still find treasures in our natural world.

I believe we can only discover what our consciousness allows us to, and when the time is 'right' then all kinds of things pop up. I believe the seeds have been here for thousands or maybe millions of years, and they are just now being discovered or noticed because we are ready, and the timing is right for us to pay attention to what they have to offer us. I'm sure you will see from the information in the book that they are quite important finds.

Recently it has come to my attention that it is time to say more about these exceptional messengers from beyond and this book is my attempt to do so.

I want to share with you how I first came into contact with these special crystals and how you can find the one that's meant for you and begin to work with it to unlock some very special energies reserved for this space and time.

# Chapter One
## More Fun in Tucson

I received my first Lemurian Seed crystal several years ago as a gift from a friend. It was made into a beautiful wand which I would use occasionally to direct energy. I could easily sense the power of the crystal, but at the time I just thought all crystals were alike.

When she gave me the wand and told me it was a 'Lemurian,' I had no idea what it was, especially since there are so many trade names associated with various stones and minerals and crystals, in particular, I didn't realize the special significance the seeds hold.

Recently I made my annual pilgrimage to the gem show in Tucson. I usually make this trip

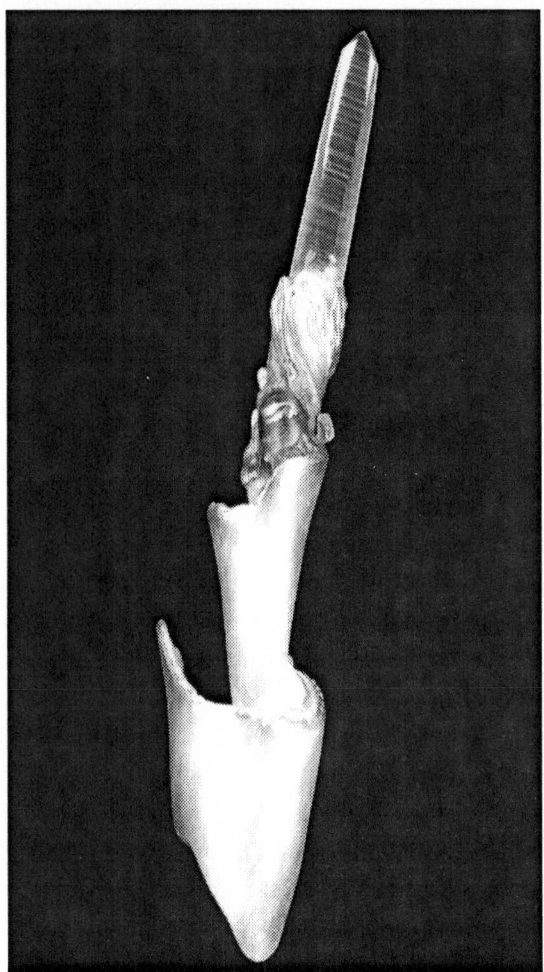

Here is the gorgeous shell wand with the Lemurian Seed crystal point. You can see orbs on the left side also!

solo, but this year I went with some long time friends who were really interested in the new Lemurian Seed Crystals they had been hearing about.

I think all things happen for a reason, so I assumed that our quest to locate them was something I should pay attention to and when we were locating vendors in the big show directory, one of the ads began to light up as I looked at it. It was one of the vendors for Lemurian Seed Crystals.

"Hey! We need to go here," I told my friends, just knowing this particular person was someone we needed to meet.

It took two days for us to finally make it over to his booth and I was officially introduced to the energy of the Lemurian Seeds, and after holding several of them I knew I would be writing another book about them, although at the time, I had no idea what it would be about.

A lot of times in the gem trade vendors rename old stones to give them new marketing potential and I have to admit when my friends first talked about 'Lemurian Seeds' I dismissed them because I assumed someone had been doing a heck of a marketing job of convincing people that they are real.

Now that I've worked with several of these, I can say with confidence that they are real and you can definitely tell the difference between the Lemurian crystals and other regular quartz crystals out there.

# Chapter Two
## How to Spot a Lemurian Seed

Not only do Lemurians stand out energetically above and beyond the rest, they also have some unique physical features that help you identify what you're looking at.

The main thing you will notice about Lemurian Seed Crystals is that they come with horizontal striations in them. In other words, it looks like there are some unusual horizontal grooves in the stones.

Each of these grooves represents a different era of time. They are records and hold information about geological time similar to the way rings on a tree trunk tell you the age of the tree.

When you hold them and run your fingers over the lines, you receive information at a deep

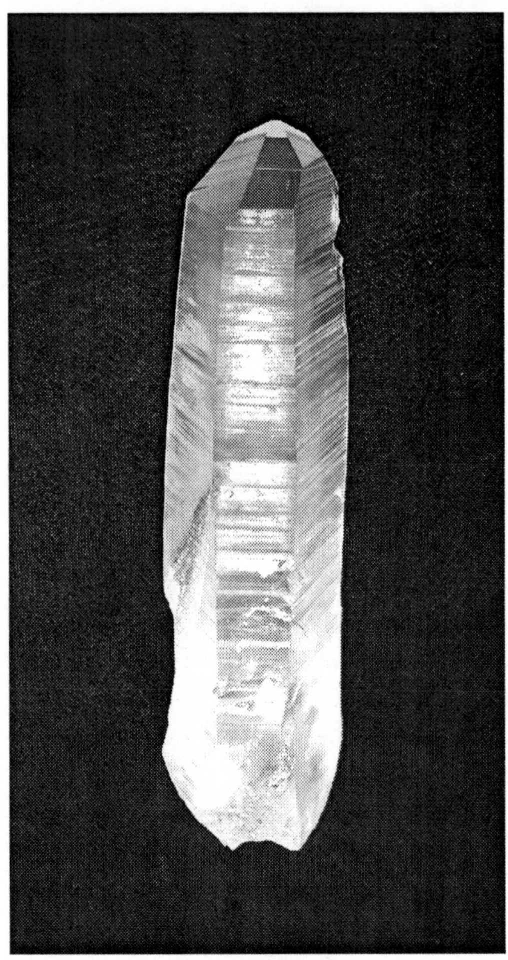

Here you can see the striations on the stone. This is a gorgeous piece!

subconscious level, like a remembrance of times past and some of this information is very valuable to all of us at this time, which is why these stones have shown up now.

The other way you tell a Lemurian is by the unusual 'keys' in them which look like big indentations on the sides of the stones. I'll have more on this later in the book and how you will use the keys.

# Chapter Three
## Location, Location, Location

Most of these crystals have been found in Brazil, and more recently there are some rare Lemurians coming out of Russia. I believe we have only touched the tip of the iceberg so to speak when it comes to finding these specimens.

Right now Brazil is the number one spot on earth for the production of gems and minerals so it would be obvious that we would find crystals there first and in the greatest quantity.

What I try to teach my students is that the mineral kingdom is so rare and valuable that when those mines are dried up they will never be exactly like that again. I do not believe they will be permanently ruined, but the point is that every specimen we receive from earth is one of a kind.

Another gorgous example...

Someday Brazil won't be the hot spot anymore and when that happens, there will be another spot and I think we will start to find more and more of these seeds because they exist all over the world. It is only a matter of time before we begin to discover them.

I wrote about this and then went off to a trip to India and Nepal recently and on the last day of my trip in Kathmandu I ran into a guy selling some stones on a table on a dirt road in the middle of the city.

I was instantly drawn to some crystals he had and as I got closer, I saw there were a half a dozen Lemurian Seeds there.

"Where did you get these?" I asked, not believing my eyes.

"Right here," he said.

"In Nepal?" I asked. He nodded.

This confirms what I have known about the seeds – that they will begin to surface in many areas. It's only a matter of time.

# Chapter Four
## Will's Crystal

A few years ago I was in Pensacola, Florida, one of my favorite spots, when my friend Will was guided to send a very special crystal home with me.

It was a huge piece of selenite with big keys (indentations) in it, and when I held it, I instantly felt an enormous download of information coming to me at a subconscious level.

The problem was the piece had several dark spots in it and I knew it needed to heal, which is what Will wanted me to do with it.

He said he got it at a shop and it was like that when he bought it and he felt I was supposed to work with it for some reason.

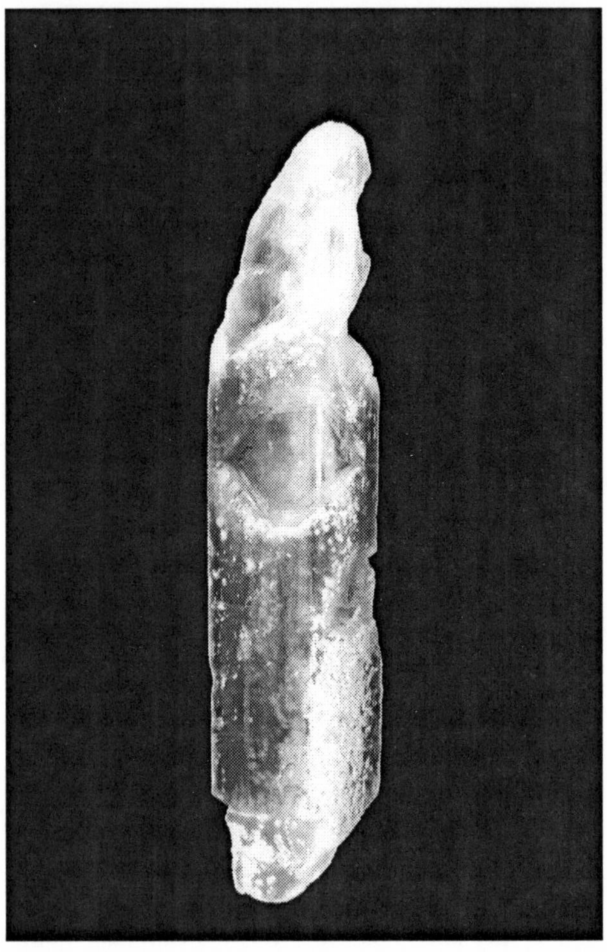

Here is Will's selenite crystal. You can see the large key in th e upper half.

I was not particularly wild about having to carry this big piece home on the plane because it is hard to get by security these days, especially with a bunch of rocks in your carry on, but regardless of any inconvenience, I knew I had to take it.

For months I did various clearings on it and it seemed to make slight improvements, becoming somewhat clearer. It was frustrating to some extent, though, because the clearing was not what I wanted it to be and it was going more slowly than I wanted. Patience is not always one of my virtues!

The stone spent the winter here in Texas and I returned it to Will the following spring. Then I went back a few months later and picked it up again, as I was guided to do, and I have had it ever since.

I told Will jokingly that I feel like we have 'joint custody' of this amazing specimen, but I knew I was to keep it longer until I understood what the message was I was to get from it, or until it healed more, or both.

When I was first coming into the energies of the Lemurian Seed Crystals at the Tucson show, I suddenly saw a vision in my mind's eye of Will's selenite specimen I had kept for three years, and I knew instantly that it too was planted by the Lemurians.

Angel shaped Selenite with Keys

Historically we have been led to believe that the seeds are only found in quartz crystals, and most of the photos you will see in the book are of quartz, but now I realized that some Lemurian Keys are also found in Selenite, which happens to be one of my favorite stones and, like quartz, it is an incredible transmitter of light.

When I realized what the purpose of the stone was, finally, after all these years, it finally began to speak to me like it had never before.

What it told me is that it comes from Lemuria and the darkness in it represents the times when the great shift happened and all was destroyed. It is coming here to heal, it told me, and that by allowing it to heal, it represented the all time notion that you can heal something today and things in the past heal simultaneously.

By being present here, as the darkness in this stone slowly lightens up, it represents a lightening of consciousness on earth and the more Lemurian Seeds that are discovered and keys activated, this stone will continue to heal, and once clear, we will already be in the age of peace. The age of peace we all know is coming.

I was so happy on my last trip to Florida to be able to tell Will about this new discovery concerning his stone! Will also gave me another piece to work with while I am writing this book that looks like an angel with wings. It is another Lemurian Selenite with dark inclusions in it and it is also promised to lighten as more seeds are activated.

# Chapter Five
## The Skull from Mount Shasta

I met some people at a show in Memphis who offered to let me commune with one of their crystal skulls. They had a table with about a dozen skulls of all sizes and all kinds of material from fluorite to amber to hematite.

I scanned them with my hand to see which ones I felt the most energy around and without a doubt, the strongest one was a smaller sample made of lava rock from none other than Mount Shasta.

I held it in my right hand, scanned it with my left hand and the store owner sent me some energy through my crown. Almost instantly I saw Shasta in my mind's eye and felt the energy of the skull.

I felt it had connections to the ancient Lemurians and saw visions of the little lemurs and could see how the size of this skull could compare to a modern day lemur.

Then I had a vision of the seed crystals in Brazil poking up from the ground, then in Russia and then my vision expanded to the entire world and I began to see lights all over the world representing all the places where the Lemurian seed crystals actually exist although nobody had found them yet. Australia, New Zealand, Polynesia Tibet, other parts of South America, India, and Africa.

When I scanned Africa, I went up toward Egypt and saw there are none in the desert there but under the Nile lining it and also under the Tigris and Euphrates in what used to be Mesopotamia now modern day Turkey the seed crystals are lining these areas to hold the consciousness of these sacred spots as the seeds of our current civilization.

Then I found myself at the Sphinx and went inside and under the ground I saw a tunnel there that fell like a mine shaft deep in the earth. It reminded me of being on a roller coaster in an amusement park. Particularly if you have ever been to Disneyland and rode on Space mountain that deep space ride where you cannot see a foot in front of you. It reminded me of that. The narrow tube fell straight down into the earth and I actually felt the sensation of falling as if on a roller coaster and at times it would level off or make a turn and then drop farther down. It was strange, to say the least. It was so real I could not recall that I was actually still sitting in the room at the show.

At one point I took a deep gulp of air and came up opened my eyes for a split second and saw I was in the room then closed them again and started up top and went through the tunnels again, only this time much faster and kept falling and falling and falling until I finally landed on the bottom in a cavern with the most amazing huge crystals I had ever seen. They had the giant keys on them like their smaller counterparts as well as the horizontal striations and instead of rubbing your hand over these, you could lean against them and layer by layer each line would reveal different information and lit up my whole being. It was truly unreal. I felt so energized and although I do not consciously know what happened with that, I felt I received almost an initiation of some kind, a download that will benefit me for the rest of my life.

Just as with the smaller versions, these striations contain data and you are like a computer just uploading this stuff only in the giant crystal cavern it was like going to the motherboard of the whole operation and becoming one with all of that. It was very profound, for sure.

I stood next to these crystals and they were taller than most buildings you see. The temperature around my body began to decrease as I felt the high frequency of these amazing giant Lemurian Seeds.

The feeling I had there in the center of the earth was one of profound grounding like I had never felt before.

This was command central for the Lemurian Seed crystals where the very first ones were planted. Just like a tree growing for thousands of years, these crystals had been there millions, even billions of years growing to unbelievable heights.

The earth lit up again from the outside and I could once more see how these original pieces and the other tiny fragments planted not just in Brazil, but all over the earth, were holding a particular frequency grid for the whole planet. It was pretty cosmic!

Have you seen those potatoes when they stick cloves in them or one of those plastic dog toys with the pointy spikes stick in and out all over it? That is what this looked like.

These interdimensional beings created such a vast network that we are only now just beginning to tap into. Over the next many years to come, more of these amazing specimens are going to be discovered by the folks who need them most. Meanwhile, they are fine where they are because they are serving purpose by just being there. The higher purpose is going to unfold as our consciousness allows us to notice more and more of them and activate other keys of consciousness to reshape our destiny.

When the woman gently patted my shoulders and told me my session was over, I was already right there with her. I had come up from the depths of the core of earth and when I opened my eyes and stood up, the soles of my feet were deeply connected to our earth like I had never experienced before, in this life anyways.

It was an awesome experience! I am grateful for the opportunity to work with the Lemurian skull.

# Chapter Six
## Brief History of Lemuria

I am always surprised at how many people still have not been familiarized with the lost civilization of Lemuria. I am sure many writers and thinkers have their own interpretations of this great civilization, so just know that this is my own version of the story, which should be as valid as any other, because the truth is none of us really knows about Lemuria except for what we recall at a soul level.

I began to hear more about Lemuria when I worked on my book Edgar Cayce's Guide to Gemstones, Minerals, Metals & More by the Edgar Cayce Foundation. Lemuria and Atlantis are such an important part of Cayce's legacy that I included a section on these stones in that book. Other than that, though, I had never been exposed to much information about Lemuria until recently.

I began to receive this information quite clearly after I started wearing a sterling silver figure of Thoth the Atlantean around my neck. I wore it because Thoth is the keeper of sacred geometry and I am currently working on a project about that subject that is quite complex.

Instead of receiving information about my other project, what I got was a two day download about the history of Lemuria and beginnings of Atlantis. Some of the information blew me away, as it was told in a way I had never heard it before with details that seemed to fill in some of the gaps for me.

So, as you read this next section, and for that matter most of the rest of this book, I will only say this is as pure as I can bring this information though tell because I am not the one telling it. For those of you who know me personally, you know I am not big on channeled writings with no scientific fact to back it up, but I am guided that this information must be put forth in this way at this time and that there is no way to substantiate it. In my mind, if you are reading this, there is some reason for that, and when I reread these passages now, I can feel the truth in them within my body so with that in mind, here goes…

Prior to the days of the dinosaurs and the Cro-Magnon man, there were two great civilizations now over 30,000 years old that predate any concepts historically accepted by the mainstream today.

As the ancient Kabbalists say, once we were all a part of the Great Spirit, just masses of energy existing out in the cosmos.

At some point in the history of creation, it was determined that a grand experiment be tried where parts of the whole would break off and experience an existence separate from everything else.

I imagine these first trials occurred on planets in other galaxies, in far off regions of space that we are currently unable to access at this time.

Planet Earth began and grew into a lush tropical space teeming with plant and insect life. Like the original concept of the Garden of Eden, Earth seemed peaceful and all things needed to sustain this peaceful life experience were available for all to share.

It was at this time the Lemurians roamed the Earth. They were peaceful, telepathic creatures filled with simplicity because there was no need for aggressive forceful ways of being.

They lived in little clans almost like furry animals, bathing, eating fresh fruit and taking care of the young. Physically they would be likened to the lemurs of Africa.

The only difference between them and the creatures of today is that they were highly intelligent and that intelligence far surpasses any other members of the animal kingdom we see today.

How could this be that these small creatures with small brains and little clawed hands could have an intelligence to create a vast and complicated world that eventually evolved into Atlantis?

It is because the Lemurians were interdimensional beings from another time and space that slipped through the space fabric looking for an inhabitable planet on which to plant the seeds for colonies throughout the galaxies.

When they came to Earth, mostly in a state we would consider to be spirit form, they looked for a peaceful creature to merge with and chose the Lemur form to work with.

It was as if they inhabited the bodies of the little creatures and took them over for a time. Living quietly and peacefully, these Lemurians spread the vibrational frequencies of love and understanding throughout the earth.

Operating in a primarily feminine energy since there was no need for conflict or struggle, and because food, water and other life necessities abounded, for thousands of years this civilization flourished.

During this time, seeds were planted all over the earth. These seeds came from another galaxy and were derived from just a few crystal molecules from other planets.

The interdimensional aspect of these beings had discovered the power of the crystals in fueling their ships, transmitting data, and stabilizing frequencies throughout the earth.

They began to mine the crystals from any planet they could, and just like we do today with trees, eventually it became apparent that these must be replenished somehow or they would become scarce.

Interdimensional scientists discovered that if they scraped just a few millimeters of crystal off of a main transmission piece, that crystal could be grown out over many years into more huge crystals, similar to the way a seed comes out of a fruit to grow a new tree.

They set up large farms throughout the galaxies and eventually decided this planet we now call Earth would be an ideal farm for their crystals which could grow out over millions of years and eventually be rediscovered and used.

Certain elders in the band of beings somehow had the ability to dip through the time stream and peek into the future.

They soon realized that by planting these crystals throughout the earth and other planets that they would be able to transmit information from their time into the future and send certain types of signals to the people of the future that would eventually save the species.

The seed crystals served as a sort of time machine, or radio, that transcended all time and could actually speak to the future races and generations, but only when consciousness was raised to a point where that would be possible.

It would take until the end of the Age of Pisces before that would happen. Prior to that, the crystals would be there, holding frequency, but they would be completely unperceivable to everyone. At the appropriate time, people would begin discovering them.

Most who will recognize these for what they are would be those people who had traveled from the past into the future. They were once the peoples of Lemuria in past incarnations, and now, having traveled to the future, they would intuitively locate these transmitters of light, activate them, and allow the loving frequencies of the past to emanate from them in times of great shifts in consciousness and turmoil, these new energies could literally be the difference between life and death of the entire planet.

As if sending a wave of love throughout the earth, the Lemurians of the past are able to communicate their intent of peace, love and healing to the entire planet simply by having these stones on earth.

The true power lies with those who choose to wake up and remember what the crystals are, where they originally planted the seeds millions of years before, and bring these up to the surface, consciously calling on them to do what they were intended to do, while allowing the keys to be unlocked so that the maximum energy can be used for the benefit of humanity during this great shift in consciousness.

Millions of years before, the Lemurian civilization had to fall. It was a part of the great plan and also a part of the balance of nature. The Lemurians, operating not from practical means, but from a place of love and highly intuitive feminine energy, were living peacefully for thousands of years but eventually the great awakener came in the form of highly masculine energy represented at that time by the dinosaurs. When dinosaurs came, it literally wiped out the peaceful space Lemurians were occupying, and yet it was the Lemurian higher consciousness that created the dinosaurs.

The shear mass of the masculine aggressive energy and the force in which these giant beings stomped the earth created so many shifts on the land that natural disasters became the norm. Earthquakes began, at that time from the outside in, as the force of those enormous creatures pounded their weight upon the earth's crust.

The majority of the Lemurians quickly disappeared. Their interdimensional hosts evacuated their shells and ascended into a state of spirit so their consciousness survived celestially.

Lemurians were not all confined by the parameters of life and death. They were able to willfully leave their bodies and ascend consciously so their knowledge was never lost.

Some of the lesser intelligent or conscious among them were physically killed and some who were mentally stronger fled to southern regions into the areas which eventually became Atlantis.

The original Lemurians were primarily situated near what is now the Pacific Rim. Where we now have the Hawaiian Islands and the areas of Polynesia and Malaysia, these beings flourished.

There are still legends in Hawaiian and Polynesian folklore about the Lost Continent of Mu, referring to Lemuria.

Today, their descendants are those same people; the beautiful round faced brown peoples of the earth.

As some of these moved out of harms way and into the new civilization which would eventually become Atlantis, there were not many left among them.

The dinosaurs reigned the earth for millions of years and during this time only the strongest among the Lemurians survived by shear willpower. The Lemurian ancestors who chose to stay had to evolve and discover new ways to kill, new weapons to use against these brutal beasts and some of the strongest survived.

The most intelligent and advanced members of this society were smart enough to create a vast underground network of tunnels and caves where they lived. It was this system that allowed any of them to survive at all. There are still rumors about these underground caves to this day and many believe the ancient ones are still living underground in areas such as Mount Shasta, California.

With the dinosaurs roaming above ground, the only way for the survivors to keep alive was to bury themselves deep in the earth and learn to survive with very little sunlight and exposure to the outside.

This was a hard existence for the species whose ancestors lived and flourished among the trees living peacefully and in concordance with all beings.

The massive amount of masculine force that created the giant dinosaurs and other creatures roaming planet Earth at this time was eventually out of balance in the natural order of things.

Life ended in a flash one fateful day as a piece of matter fell from the sky and completely wiped out the reptilian dinosaur species.

The only survivors of this catastrophic event were the brave survivors who lived underground. After the destruction, they slowly came back to the earth's surface and saw the sunlight again.

They noticed the pounding force of the giants who once towered above their underground homes were no longer there, shaking the walls and foundations, and because of that, they were finally safe to come up for air.

# Chapter Seven
## Fall of Lemuria

At this time, the shock felt round the galaxy attracted the attention of many beings from far away places. Those who were blessed with technology came to assist in the rebuilding of the planet we now call Earth because they felt they could have a stronghold in the recreation of this new civilization and that because it was filled with natural resources such as the crystals and gold needed for their technology, to assist in the rebuilding was of benefit to all who joined in. It was the early exploitation of the natural resources of Earth.

Today, we think we are just now exploiting what Mother Earth has to offer, yet this type of exploitive energy has been on our planet for millions of years. Ours has always been one of the most valuable planets so rich and abundant in resources that all who see it have always wanted a piece of what we have here.

The crystals are the primary tool for communication and transmission, teleportation and information technology. In the 21st century, some of those who have pushed the technologies to the edge of what our minds can grasp are actually just time travelers who come to us from times past remembering most consciously what they used to know back then. It seems so easy now for us to simply think of something and then there it is. That is a form of time travel where the conscious interdimensional ones are simply here again, bringing that knowledge to us.

In those days, the crystals were necessary, but so was the gold. Gold was used in special linings and plates used inside ships that enabled them to rip across galaxies and through different dimensional spaces, black holes and asteroid belts at lightning speed and enabled survival to occur. Without the higher frequencies of gold for protection, men could easily get burned up when crossing dimensions and so the gold was necessary and also quite rare.

In a way similar to planting crystal seeds, these early pioneers also planted gold molecules but soon realized they were only conducive to certain types of atmospheres such as that found on planet earth which is why earth has always been such an important factor in the history of the universe.

Crystals could thrive in a more diverse set of conditions, but gold was much more precious.

Although it is found in other areas planets and galaxies, earth is still considered among the crown jewels of creation for her ability to maintain the energy required to cultivate gold.

Just when we think we will run out of gold, it is, after all, a natural resource, but we will never run out of it because interdimensional beings are continually planting these seeds to enable earth to regenerate gold for the rest of this planet's existence because it is not only necessary for our survival, but for the survival of so many other planets in this galaxy and beyond which mankind is currently totally unaware of. We must continue to plant these seeds as a guarantee we will all survive.

At the higher levels of consciousness those who are continually visiting the earth now, unseen by so many who are what we could call 'sleepers' we higher beings will continue to visit earth, plant the necessary seeds to allow this planet and all in the galaxy to survive.

# Chapter Eight
## A Special Message

This brings an interesting state of mind to the forefront. There is this continual fear on earth that things will run out, that supplies will dry up and that it all will go away.

This is simply not the case at all. As long as one drop of any resource remains, the hologram of that will allow others to multiply it and it will always be a part of our creation. Earth will never run out of water, fuel or anything.

If you would like less smoke and pollution, yes, you should think of these 'alternative' ways of doing things although you should know that these are not alternative at all but the ideas are things used in the past and those who have them are time travelers from then coming to now to attempt to get the planet to move forward.

The current ways of doing these things are so outdated and they really need to be revised. In the evolution of the human species we have come to use the fossil fuels and now that needs to evolve. It is energetically necessary for this to happen to complete the cycle of what lies ahead in the future.

Human beings are not dying off and are not running out of things. Your spirit is recycled from the Great One Spirit and when you perish in your current form you will come back again and again and when you allow the technology to evolve as it must, you are allowing the space in the future to exist.

It is the future you have already created for yourselves, although you may or may not be aware of it. Start to imagine it, as you say, and you will see that everything you worry about is silly and unnecessary.

All is as it should be, there is no shortage or lack in this universe, but things must change and evolve so stop trying to hang on to the old ways. Think of it as driving a car. Just allow it and you will be okay. Get in the car and go down the road.

Notice what you pass by and notice what interests you and enjoy it. Learn from it and see how you can use that to recreate the future so you won't have to go where the dinosaurs did. You will allow yourselves to be and do and know everything that has ever happened and all that is yet to come because it is all right now, after all.

# Chapter Nine
## Message Concerning The Keys

As I began to come in contact with the special crystals, I was told they had keys in them, which I told you earlier are like big inclusions.

The keys usually look like strange multilayered indentions within these crystals. You can activate these keys by putting your finger inside of them and instantly they will offer the subconscious download of whatever information the crystal contains.

Some of these crystals are there to simply hold a frequency of love, for example. By holding the crystal and putting your finger in the key, your soul will unlock the most primitive and pure frequency of the love vibration man has ever known of. Like stepping back through the ages to the time

This photo looks like modern art!

of advanced feminine peaceful loving energies, these crystals will heal a section of your soul through remembrance and reflection at levels you may not consciously understand.

Here is where more special information will be shared:

The other crystals may actually hold keys of instruction. Information you are supposed to disseminate to others, creations or inventions you are to build which are not really 'inventions' after all, because these are things already built in times past which you are called to remember and recreate in the now.

So you will do it simply by placing your finger in the key. You may not even consciously know how you have acquired such skill, such imagination and inspiration. For so many of you it will be unconscious.

Like a dream, the thought will flood your mind, yet this thought comes with motivation to act upon it and by acting you will bring the thing out of your mind, out of your imagination and put it into the realm of the living. You will create and you will not realize that by creating you have actually recreated something that has already been.

So good for you, Creator. Enjoy what you are doing, enjoy the accolades of what others tell you about what you created and be glad you have the gift of listening to your soul and the messages from ancestors who have come before you.

Let this light shine through you and the wisdom you have to share will enlighten and enliven others who may also need your information in order that they too may become inspired to create what they are called to do in their lifetimes.

It will all work out splendidly, as you will see in time. You must simply find those crystals with the keys you are destined to unlock and do that and then do not fear moving forward in it.

Just know you are destined to do these great things and by so doing you are helping the all of humanity to move out of this state of fear and into this new state of being, creating and doing as if you are moving down a boat in a river, you let ideas and thoughts flow from you, through you and to others and you do not get concerned about it, you allow it. You get out of your own way and allow so that you and humanity at large can enjoy it and know that this is what is meant to be.

Of course you may think all of this sounds ridiculous, that you are simply imagining all that is being said to you, but on some deeper level, your soul is listening to me and knowing that what I am saying is nothing but truth, pure truth, simply put, this is what has come to pass and what you hold now are the keys to remember that and to take the best of that and move into a better future. Are you willing to listen so you may hear what you are to do?

Good. That is all you need to be is ready to receive it. That is all. Ready and willing and open to what awaits you. You are open and powerful. You should not take on airs or become conceited that you are better than others of your kind, you aren't.

Your gift is your openness. You are willing to hear things that others chose to ignore and because of this you are special. Others can do what you can do only they are afraid. They see you and wish they could be like you, and they can, in their own ways, but their fears, which are unfounded, are limiting what they are able to do.

They could hold a crystal, unlock the keys within and hear or feel what they are to do, but they would allow their minds to override their hearts and would not follow that innate guidance within.

Then they wonder why their lives are so shallow, so incomplete and so miserable. Then they look upon you and they see all you have and they show jealousy toward you for all you have that they do not.

They want to chastise you and cut you down. They want to tell you you're wrong and your ideas are too foolish, too naïve, to selfless to ever work in a world like the one we live in, and to a certain point, they cause you to wonder if they are right because your mind then begins to question all you have thought about, all you are and all you are becoming.

Promise yourself you will not allow this to happen to you. You must keep those, as you call them, rose colored glasses on. You must allow the magic to happen in your life and see the good in others despite what others want you to see, think and believe.

This is your reality and you are the one who is creating this moment by moment with your thoughts and actions so continue to seek only your own counsel and continue to know within yourself what you must do to find peace and happiness.

Only you can know what those things mean to you and you must follow your own bliss, your own path to peace. You can do or have anything your heart desires if you just remember this. Keep your course on track and believe in goodness. It is always the higher ground.

# Chapter Ten
## 12 Keys of Life

The Lemurian Seed Crystals have keys in them which were briefly mentioned earlier. These are the keys that were imbedded in the consciousness of the Lemurian Seed Crystals.

Each crystal has one of these 12 Keys of Life encoded into it so when the user unlocks the information, one of these codes of consciousness will be instantly downloaded into their DNA and passed down from generation to generation.

Sometimes you may know which one of the keys you are working with and other times you will only receive the information on the astral or interdimensional level.

It won't matter though, because energetically it will already be transferred into the user's body so future people can know it more consciously.

You have done many experiments lately on the power in water and how your thoughts affect the shapes of water molecules and this technology was something transferred to your consciousness from Lemurian forefathers. It is through this same idea that the seed crystals are able to transfer their keys to people whether conscious of it or not.

Because the crystals are comprised of water, much like the human body, when the crystal key is opened, it is designed to release the holographic impression of one of the 12 keys to the user by imbedding that holographic thought form into the water molecules in the key holder's body.

When this transfer of energy is complete, the water molecules begin to reshape the outer structure of the body and the internal cells and eventually the DNA molecules themselves. In that way, the people who eventually give birth to others will be able to inherently pass this information off to their offspring and on to future generations of humanity.

The time is now for this transmission to occur and that is why these crystals have been discovered and will continue to be discovered for the next several years. The Lemurians of past knew they would have to plant enough seeds with high frequency thought transmissions in forms of the Keys or 12 Truths that enough people could find them, activate them and eventually cause the shift in consciousness that so many have predicted for this period in time.

Experiments on meditation show what I mean by this. If enough people meditate in an area you have already discovered that the crime rates go down, there are fewer accidents and more peace abounds in the vicinity of the meditation area. This is the same concept. If enough people find and activate the keys to the 12 truths, then these will not only affect the key holder, but the several square mile radius around the crystal and eventually there will be enough activated for a complete enlightenment, as you call it, of all on your planet.

You have known the experiments with the monkeys and the fact that as one learns to wash fruit and teaches another, once 100 monkeys learn it then the idea spreads to the other side of the world instantly and all monkeys wash fruit.

Lemurian seeds will go beyond this 100 into the thousands so there will be no doubt the shift will occur quickly and will be permanent.

The higher love frequency vibrations emitted by these crystals will totally lend to and assist in the Great Shift your elders have predicted.

These indigenous tribal elders who share this wisdom with the world do so because they are the direct descendants of the ancient Lemurians and have consciously decided to assist humanity at this time by time traveling in their near Lemurian forms into today's world to be the truth bringers for all humanity.

# Chapter Eleven
## Keys Revealed

# Key 1
### You are made of love

When you were first created you were nothing but love, a frequency vibration in the cosmos and although you find yourself now in body, on a physical planet and with what you believe are physical concerns, you unknowingly perceive yourself falsely as something with boundaries and limitations when all you really are is a unique expression of the vibration of love.

When you remember you are love and begin to emanate this out to your fellow creatures on earth, you actually create a change in the world.

Be love and see how others respond t you.

Other emotions are masks and illusions for what you really are so just remember you are made of love.

# Key 2

## You are a time traveler from the past, present and future

You are from the same time and space as I am. You are from the past. You helped plant the seeds you now wish to find and decode and when you do and you unlock the love and the higher ideals and inspirations contained within, you will in fact affect the future of mankind, a future that you are already participating in although you may not always be consciously aware of it.

Anytime you are about to take an action, I want you to imagine you can go out into your future and see the consequences of said action and how you are affecting those around you. When you do this you will have a more conscious experience of your future and the fact that you are from the future.

When you hold a key in your hand I want you to imagine you can go back to the moment that key or seed was planted and use what you call your imagination to think of what was intended by planting this seed.

When you do that you will remember in a far away space when you planted this seed yourself so that the you from today, from right now, could find it and experience what you call enlightenment.

This is a word that actually means remembrance. You will recall the higher ideal way of being and you will allow yourself to go there and be with that energy for the betterment of all.

When you allow this by remembering a past you cannot quite recall and going to a future you cannot quite grasp, you are living the second key which is acknowledging your soul's birthright as a citizen in the cosmic destiny, a time traveler, a messenger of peace for all time.

# Key 3

## You are creating your reality by thought deed and action

Remember that every time you think, feel and do, your surroundings will reflect that. If you want to be love, then you must think it first.

If you want to feel prosperous, you must first feel it as if it is with you and it will be. It is that simple.

There is no lack anywhere. You have the ability with your mind to reshape your world to whatever way suits you and when you do so by recalling past, and remembering future with love, you are changing the world.

That is your mission. That is your highest purpose.

A stunning example of a key

# Key 4

## You are living in an abundant world where there is no lack of anything

There is no lack. You have mistakenly been living in a time of darkness and limitation which you created and planned for in the past so you could learn your lessons at a higher level.

You would occasionally take things for granted so in the past you created the space where an energy of lack could prevail so when you found the keys and once again recalled the past, you could have a deeper understanding of the meaning of what it is to have everything you need and be in a world where prosperity abounds.

When you set this love energy in motion, the love that you are, you unlock the door to knowing that your heart's desires are only a thought away.

Stop dwelling on what you do not have and start recalling that you have everything you already need. Just remember what you have as if it is already with you and you will draw it to you in time.

# Key 5

## You can have anything you want simply by believing you can

What is it that you want to create for yourself? Have you stopped to think of what that is? You think you have such a lack of everything yet you fail to monitor your thoughts and feelings and realize you are getting everything you think about.

If you think of reasons to be fearful, you create those things in your life that show you those fearful experiences. If you think you have no one to love you, you create that. If you think you have not enough to eat, or money to take you places, you create that too.

Why can't you begin to believe you have enough money, enough love, enough stuff and then begin to notice how it shows up for you.

It does when you are able to be love, to remember your past and recall your future where you know you have it all right now. Be that today and watch your life unfold for you.

Watch how you can heal others by showing them all that is possible through the power of belief. Do it today for yourself and for all who live at this time.

Your presence is like a key for others to help them see visually how the work is done. You believe it and others believe you and they begin to also transform the way they see life and possibility.

All is possible. Just do it! Now is the time!

# Key 6

## You are changing the lives of thousands of others just by your presence on earth at this time

When you are present and in your loving state of remembrance, your presence on this earth is affecting thousands of others simultaneously.

You are saying 'yes,' but I do not know thousands so how is that possible?'

It is possible because by knowing dozens you shine your light to them and they are happier and more loving and they go into the world and spread that to the dozens they know and those people are affected and they go to the dozens they know and so on.

It is true that one drop of water affects all else on this plane because it is nothing but a field of possibility, an illusion, and when you consciously and lovingly act in this illusion in a higher way, it will affect everything else.

# Key 7

## You are positive and happy and by being that way, you spread this joy to others who are around you

Your loving ways are spread through this field to the others who you meet and interact with on a daily basis.

You will not always know how your presence is affecting these you just need to know that you do affect others.

By showing them the way, by sharing possibility for happiness and peace with them, you are spreading it throughout the world.

Be it and allow others to imitate it.

# Key 8

## You are able to listen to your heart which tells you everything you need to know

It is your heart, not your brain or mind that tells you what is true, right and just and it is from the heart you should make your decisions on what it is you need to be doing and experiencing at this time.

Do not allow your mind to override the feelings of your heart and soul because only disaster can follow.

Ask for your body and mind to open to the love vibration you are and always work from within this frame of reference and you will be well and your life will be blessed as you bless others with that presence. That is your duty, your purpose at this time. Love, be loved and ask your own heart for guidance. You cannot consult with another's heart because only you know what you need to be doing. So do it, and do it with joy.

# Key 9

## You cannot change others only yourself

You have to awaken your own self to your love vibration and do all you can to be in that space as much as your illusory world will allow.

You can change your response to others your reactions to stimulus and what you want to do, say or think about things that come to you.

When you change how you respond, in that, others are automatically forced to change and become different and through that there is peace that will abound.

You cannot change others and yet you can change them by changing the waves of frequency you are sending out then others have to respond differently to you and in that you have changed yourself and them.

The thing is they are also you and you are

them because the separate nature is only an illusion. But within this illusion remember you change the part of it represented by you in order to give others the space needed to make the change in a way they feel empowered by and everyone wins.

# Key 10

## You have a purpose for being and by following your path, you help others follow theirs

When you come to this earth plane and you tap into your love frequency and recall past, visualize humanities future, you are living purposely and by doing so your purpose shines to others as a living example and they are able to become what they are meant to become simply because your spirit is allowing them the space, by not trying to change them directly, so they may also follow their own unique path and live their purpose as well.

If you do not show people how it is done by living your higher purpose, others cannot know how to do it and will not do it because someone has to set a space for allowing others to be their highest potential.

That is your purpose.

Following heart, being love and allowing the keys of life to unfold for you daily is helping all beings.

Isn't this beautiful?

# Key 11

## You are made up of every thought deed and action that came before you and will come after you

You are a byproduct of your ancestors from the earliest times as well as your own souls incarnations and all of the things you have already created in the future by the thought waves you are sending out today. Every thought and action today is creating the future that currently exists in a future dimension of space time.

You are being this today and in the past and always and who you are right now, the way you think, dress and look, is a sum total of all the moments of creation come together in the right now.

You can change this in an instant if it is not what you want by simply changing your mind and increasing your love frequency.

You are all that is as is everyone else.

# Key 12

## You can change yourself and when you do, you change the whole world and every other world in existence for now and for all eternity

To think that if you increase this love vibration now that you are only affecting yourself is just not true.

You are affecting yourself, the others who you see now on your planet and you are also affecting every other place in every other galaxy and space time continuum that exists or will ever exist.

What you choose to do, think and say in this lifetime is like a marker in space. You leave your mark on every world in every time.

So many of you are so concerned with leaving a legacy, or leaving a visible mark on your society but what you cannot understand is that just by being you have already left your mark.

If you cannot see it, it is reflected by the

more visible things left by others who you indirectly assisted along the way. You did not recall that the smile you gave or the help you offered to someone in need was actually rippling throughout time and affecting everyone in all time throughout the ages in past, present and future.

You bought a meal, changed a tire, took someone to the doctor and you thought no more of it. You had no idea the effect your one action had on all others around you.

To the person who received it who may offer help to someone else in the future, to those who saw you render aid who did similar things for others and so on.

It is a chain reaction because you are all linked. All people, all creatures and things of earth are linked to all others in all times in all galaxies in all universes.

Do not think you are small and insignificant and without value. You have more value than you can even imagine from where you are standing today. You must understand it and understand the magnitude for why you are here and be okay with it.

Know it and know you have purpose, mission and reason for being so get to it.

Start to hear the voice of your heart and

follow what it tells you because all time is depending on you to offer your piece of the puzzle because without all the pieces coming together the whole cannot be complete.

You have great value and do not underestimate yourself and what you have come here to do. You have to start now and step one day at a time to get there.

Know what you perceive as delay or difficulty is represented by things you cannot see from your vantage point and know that they are necessary.

Your highest purpose is not to fear them or be angered by them but to see them as necessary delays or bumps that allow every other thing to be as it is written in the records and as it should be. You are the player in the orchestra of life and you have control over your own instrument but not completely over the whole orchestra.

Just play your part and do what you can to harmonize with the other players. You may not understand the notes they chose or why they play at that speed.

Just accept it as part of a bigger piece you cannot comprehend from your seat in the pit and go with it and do your part for the whole and betterment for all.

Even a beautiful symphony has dark parts to balance the light. You must allow for both to exist in the delicate balance of what you are attempting to create.

# Chapter 12
## How to work with your Lemurian

I assume if you are reading this then you are one of the thousands who are called to work with these special crystals at this time. If so, I want to offer some guidelines to working with your Lemurian Seed Crystals.

First off, I do believe these stones choose you, you do not choose them. I have talked about this to a certain extent in my other books, but here I mean this on a much deeper level. You are really the chosen one, if you will, who is supposed to press the key and unlock the hidden energetic frequencies offered by the stone you feel called to purchase.

If a stone comes to you, know it is meant to be. If you are in an area where some are offered, it is often challenging to decide which one is for you and which is not.

I usually say pick the first one you come to. I want to amend that by saying there is another step to that process.

I have noticed the past few years that when I encounter a stone I really like I am inclined to buy it. Or at least that's how I used to be. Now I hold it for a moment and see if it is going to download information to me. Normally, it does.

If it does, then I see if this is a continual ongoing thing or if I have learned everything from this piece that I need to and if I have, I leave it for someone else. So now I often buy the second one that comes to me – not always, of course, but sometimes.

I think that when I speak to the stones they all tell me whatever I need to know at that time. That does not mean that I always am meant to have an ongoing relationship with the stone.

That would be like thinking everyone you run into is someone you need to have a relationship with. Just because you meet someone, they may share important information with you that may change your life, but sometimes this information can be received in just a few minutes and does not take long at all.

Maybe what the stone offers is a clue so

when you do pick up the stone you are supposed to work with you will know it and you will be enriched by what the previous stone shared.

In fact, had it not been for your short communion with that other stone, you may not even be prepared to receive what the other is offering you.

Think about this, if you will, especially in the quest for your Lemurian Seed Crystal. Please do not get too bogged down with this though!

I want you to remember that you have a very powerful innate intelligence within you and you need to ask your higher self what to do and know you are correct!

I know you will do the best you can and you do not need to ask me or anyone else what to do, just do it!

# Chapter 13

## Unlocking the Keys

As far as working with the crystal once you have it, if yours has a key, then you need to hold it in your hand. I like to hold mind in my left hand, but you may be different so just notice what feels good to you.

Then I take my index finger on my right hand and put it in the key and hold it there. You will feel a rush of energy run through you that you won't believe! Again, just use the hand and finger you feel most comfortable with.

My giant keyed crystal seems to like to be held firmly in my left hand with my left thumb in the key. I have another one though that needs my index finger in it in just a certain way. If I don't have it exactly that way, it won't download properly.

You need to think of this like a security device that is ready to read your fingerprint. Like one of those futuristic laser devices that only seeks you and your fingerprint for activation.

When you get it right, you will know it so what I want to say is you have to hold these and figure out which way is best for that particular seed. I think they might be different for each one so experiment a bit!

Pretend you are a safecracker and you have a set of 12 keys – two hands and ten fingers – and you have to find the exact combination that will unlock the treasure, which in this case is the download of one of the 12 keys of consciousness described earlier in the book.

Just follow your innate intuition and all will be well! Eventually these keys will be activated and the shift to higher frequencies will be completed.

# Chapter Fourteen
## Conclusion

As we prepare for what some call the end times, I would like you to consider that what may be coming to an end is an era, a way of being, and that we are actually about to come into a period of greater enlightenment and knowledge and peace that we have ever known before.

Our thoughts and actions are more important than ever, and to me, part of that means we must stay positive and realize that the world we have been dreaming of, the world of peace, tranquility and prosperity are actually within our reach.

If enough people can hold these peaceful thoughts and ways of being, then by doing so, our entire species is allowed to evolve and expand to new heights far greater than we could ever have previously imagined.

Now is the time for you to do whatever you can do to assist in this transition to higher realms of light and peace.

One way to assist is by asking how you may serve and by allowing yourself to become one of the thousands of people who will discover and unlock the keys the ancient Lemurians left for us to discover at this time.

Ask that the highest intention come forth from these crystals and notice how this peace emanates from you and around you and out into the world.

How can you, one person, make a difference in such a big place as our known universe?

You can do it simply by being and knowing that one drop of water affects the entire ocean.

## *Ab Uno Disce Omnes*

***From One Person Learn All People***

# Bibliography

Balibar, Francoise. *The Science of Crystals.* Poughkeepsie, New York: McGraw-Hill, Inc., 1993.

Bauer, Max. *Precious Stones: A Popular Account of Their Characters, Occurrence, and Applications, with an Introduction to Their Determination, for Mineralogists, Lapidaries, Jewellers, etc.* Rutland, Vermont: Charles E. Tuttle Company, 1969.

Bullis, Douglas. *Crystals: The Science, Mysteries and Lore.* New York, NY: Crescent Books, 1990.

Campbell, Dan. *Edgar Cayce on the Power of Color, Stones and Crystals.* New York, NY: Warner Books, 1989.

Cayce, Edgar Evans. *Mysteries of Atlantis Revealed: The Century's Greatest Psychic Confronts One of the World's Oldest Mysteries.* New York, NY: St. Martin's Press, 1997, 1988..

Finster, Elaine. *"Larimar Coming to America: The Story of Larimar."* Crystal Pathways Magazine, Volume II Issue I, Summer 1989.

Harris, Stephen L. *Agents of Chaos: Earthquakes, Volcanoes and Other Natural Disasters*. Missoula, Montana: Mountain Press Publishing Company, 1990.

Hulse, David Allen. *The Key of It All: An Encyclopedic Guide to the Sacred Languages & Magickal Systems of the World – Book One: The Eastern Mysteries*. St. Paul, MN: Llewellyn Publications, 1993.

Hulse, David Allen. *The Key of It All: An Encyclopedic Guide to the Sacred Languages & Magickal Systems of the World – Book Two: The Western Mysteries.* St. Paul, MN: Llewellyn Publications, 1994.

Kaehr, Shelley. *Edgar Cayce's Guide to Gemstones, Minerals, Metals & More*. Virginia Beach, VA: ARE Press, 2005.

Kaehr, Shelley. *Gemstone Journeys*. Dallas, TX: Out of This World Publishing, 2003.

King, Godfre Ray. *Unveiled Mysteries*. Schaumburg, IL: Saint Germain Press, 1982.

Kirkpatrick, Sidney D. *Edgar Cayce: An American Prophet.* New York, NY: Riverhead Books, 2000.

Kunz, George Frederick. *The Curious Lore of Precious Stones*. New York, NY: Dover Publications, 1913.

Liddicoat, Jr., Richard T. *Handbook of Gem Identification.* Santa Monica, CA: Gemological Institute of America, 1977.

Mottana, Annibale. *Simon & Schuster's Guide to Rocks & Minerals.* New York, NY: Fireside Books, 1977.

Schumann, Walter. *Gemstones of the World.* New York, NY: Sterling Publishing Co., Inc., 2000.

*Scientific Properties and Occult Aspects of Twenty-Two Gems, Stones, and Metals: A Comparative Study Based on the Edgar Cayce Readings.* Virginia Beach, VA: ARE Press, 1960.

Stemman, Roy. *Atlantis and the Lost Lands.* London: The Danbury Press, Inc. 1976.

Zim, Herbert S. and Paul Shaffer. *Rocks & Minerals: A Guide to Familiar Minerals, Gems, Ores and Rocks.* New York, NY: Simon & Schuster, 1957.

## About the Author

Shelley Kaehr, Ph.D. has had a lifelong love affair with gems and minerals.

She grew up in the Southwestern US and originally sparked her interest with stones through her parents.

As an adult, she had a synchronistic encounter with a Native American shaman whotaught her the healing properties of gems and minerals. SHe published these techniques in her first book on stones called Gemstone Journeys.

In 2005, Shelley's bestselling book Edgar Cayce's Guide to Gemstones was published through the Edgar Cayce Foundation Press highlighting the stones Cayce mentioned in his life readings including those found in the periodic table of the elements, Biblical stones and stones of the lost civilizations of Lemuria and Atlantis.

Her last book on stones, Divination of God, describes the Urim and Thummim and the Breastplate of the High Priest found inthe book of Exodus.

For more information, visit her online at

**www.shelleykaehr.com**

# NOTES

# NOTES

CPSIA information can be obtained at www.ICGtesting.com
Printed in the USA
LVOW11s1527270614

391884LV00004B/5/A